When the wicked came upon me to devour my flesh, my enemies and foes stumbled and fell.

Psalm 27:2

SCARS OF SURVIVAL

MY JOURNEY DURING AND AFTER BREAST CANCER

SHELIA P. MOSES

Library of Congress Cataloging-in-Publication Date: Scars of Survival: My Journey During and After Breast Cancer

Contact Information

Shelia P. Moses @ shelia@mosesbooks.com

Website: sheliapmoses.com

ISBN: 9798862126709

CONTENTS

Introduction

Chapters

DEDICATION

This book is dedicated to my big sister,

Dr. Loraine Moses Stewart and my niece, Ronnetta Moses.

INTRODUCTION

I have written twenty-seven books in my lifetime. I believe this is my most important story because I feel in my heart that this book will help someone. It is my prayer that sharing my journey during and after breast cancer will benefit millions of women and men around the world. It's the story you know too well because you or someone you love might have had or have breast cancer. You might be going through a health challenge as you are reading this book. Maybe you just started or just finished chemotherapy. Whatever your situation might be, I hope that your questions will be answered while reading *Scars of Survival: My Journey During and After Breast Cancer.*

Women and men of all races and backgrounds have heard the frightening words, "You have breast cancer." Yes, men can have breast cancer. I know that people feel afraid and lost when they receive the news. There is also a sense of feeling alone, no matter how big your family might be or how many friends you have. Some people have an army of supporters, but others truly are alone. Whether you have a huge village or you are alone, I want all of you to know that there is life after breast cancer. It is not a cake walk but a walk with God, and you can get to the other side.

The second objective of this book is to serve as an alarm clock. I am referring to the alarm of awareness regarding your body. I want my journey to wake you up if you are ignoring a sign that your body is trying to send you to tell you that something is wrong. I am grateful every day that I did not ignore the signs. I am only alive because I followed the instincts God gave me.

There is a long history of breast cancer in my family. Four of my mother's siblings had a daughter with breast cancer. My mother was not excluded from this club. She, too, would eventually have not one but two daughters join this war. A war that only God can help you win. When we found out that my sister Loraine had breast cancer, it never clearly registered with me that a second sister would have the same fate. That was the first mistake. Not only did the lightning of cancer strike twice with siblings but a third time with my beloved niece, Ronnetta, who lost her battle to breast cancer in 2007. She was only 34 years old.

With all the stories that did not have a happy ending in my family and families around the world, I want to share my story that did *not* end in sadness. I am not a doctor, so I have no medical advice to give you. What I offer you in this book is my journey from the day I heard the words, "I am sorry, Ms. Moses, but you have breast cancer," to the day I heard, "You are cancer free." I want to share tips on how I discovered my breast cancer after the mammogram and ultrasound reports said that I was fine. I am delighted to share tips I received from Civil Rights icon, comedian and health guru Dick Gregory. Most of all, I want to share my journey to keep the faith and my walk with God during the worst time of life. A walk that I not only survived but thrived. I want the same for you!

SCARS OF SURVIVAL

CHAPTER 1

FINDING OUT

There are moments in our lives that we never forget. One of those moments for me happened on June 1, 2015. I will never forget when and how I found out that I had breast cancer. I will never forget the physical and emotional feeling that came over my entire body. The fear of confirming what I already knew, but had taken two months to confirm, was earthshaking.

The first sign that something was wrong was so very clear to me. In early April 2015, I didn't feel sick; I just felt different. My body was sending me a signal that something was not only wrong but that it was serious. My mother had many old sayings that I live by, one of which is: "Your first mind is your right mind." Hearing her say that all my life led me to a habit of listening to my first instincts.

So, when I started feeling almost odd, I was listening to my body talk to me. As the days went by, I continued to feel tired all the time and my energy was very low.

What I knew for sure was that before April 2015, I had only experienced a few minor health challenges in my 53 years on earth. In 1995 I had laparoscopic surgery to remove fibroid tumors, and in 2000 I had surgery on my neck to remove a lymphoma. I also had a benign cyst removed from my right breast in 2001. All three were outpatient surgeries.

Until I walked into Nova Alexandria Hospital on November 18, 2015, to have a double mastectomy, I had never spent a single night in a hospital. The most time I had slept in any hospital was with my mother. I had slept at my mother's bedside over and over again, but never as a patient. That's it! I was a perfectly healthy woman.

I had always made it my business to get my annual physical and pap examinations. I started getting mammograms in 1993, at age 32, after discovering a mass the size of a quarter in my right breast.

I was living in Atlanta at the time and I immediately went to see my physician when I discovered the mass. It was very round and I could physically move it with my hand. My physician was alarmed and insisted I get a mammogram immediately. I am telling you this story to help all the women who have been told that they don't need a mammogram until they are 40 years old. My first mammogram showed that I had dense tissue. My physician was not satisfied with the dense tissue report so she referred me to a great breast specialist in her building, Dr. Debra Martin.

Even in the early 1990s, Dr. Martin was not comfortable with the notion of not doing further testing on patients with dense tissue. She had all the equipment in her office and she did a sonogram. Dr. Martin's new test showed that I indeed had a cyst in the area the mammogram was showing only as dense tissue. The results were my first lesson in having fine doctors who believe in sending you to a specialist for further testing. Dr. Martin performed a needle biopsy that included draining all the fluid from the mass. She told me she would be in touch with the results in a few days. When I left her office, I noticed the cyst was totally gone.

As promised, her nurse called me a few days later and told me the test results showed the cyst was benign. She also informed me that Dr. Martin wanted to see me again in six months. I went back in six months, and after that, I had annual visits with Dr. Martin around the same time as with my primary care physician.

A few years later, a cyst came back in the same location in my right breast and Dr. Martin performed a needle biopsy. Once again, all the fluid was removed and the cyst disappeared. Fast forward to 2000; the cyst returned in the same location. Dr. Martin insisted that I have outpatient surgery and not a needle biopsy. The hospital sent her the results and once again the news was good. No CANCER! I continued my annual mammograms followed by a sonogram. Getting a sonogram is always a battle with the insurance company, but it's worth the peace of mind, even when I have to pay out of pocket. From 2000 until 2015, I didn't have any problems with the cysts returning. Once I decided to relocate closer to home, I made one final visit to see all of my doctors. I moved to Alexandria, Virginia in 2014 believing that I was in good health. I usually do all my exams around my birthday in July, so I was not thinking about new doctors until I started feeling bad in mid-April 2015. My intention was to ask one of my friends in the D.C. area for recommendations, but I had not found the time to do that. I had to speed that process up when I felt a hard mass in my left breast while in the shower. I was rushing to a school visit but I couldn't stop thinking about how hard the mass in my breast felt. It had suddenly appeared out of nowhere. Strangely, it was in the left breast this time, not the right where I had found cysts three times in the past. The cysts had always been round and hard, but not as hard as the new cyst. No... this was definitely different. It didn't hurt but I could feel the pressure when I touched it.

I was so concerned that I went into the bathroom when I arrived at school and felt the mass again. As I was leaving the school, I had to check out at the front desk and noticed the nurse was sitting in her office next door. I knocked on her door and told her about the mass I found. She was the first angel God sent me on what was about to turn into the longest, hardest journey of my life. I told her that I was fairly new to the area and needed a primary care doctor and an OB/GYN. I knew that I would need a referral from a physician or OB/GYN if I needed a specialist. She referred me to a physician but told me to ask for a referral to see Dr. Barry Rothman.

I prefer going to a female OB/GYN but I didn't want to go to a total stranger. The nurse knew this doctor so at least there was some connection. By the grace of God, I followed my instincts again and went to the OB.GYN she referred me to after getting the referral from the physician.

Dr. Rothman was not only a good doctor but a great listener. After he examined me in late April 2015, Dr. Rothman told me he definitely felt something and we were not taking any chances due to my family history. He referred me to a radiologist, but they didn't have an appointment until the next week.

On April 30, 2015, I walked into the Alexandria Radiologist on Seminary Road in Alexandria, Virginia for what I prayed would be good news. When I arrived, the ladies at the front desk were really nice and professional. I learned quickly that the kindness of the people you see first when you are embarking on a medical journey is important to your mental and physical well-being.

First up was a mammogram! The radiologist was just the opposite of the woman at the front desk. She didn't talk much and my concerns were not hers. After my mammogram, she came back with my results and casually told me that I had dense tissue. I told her that I was concerned due to my family history and the dense tissue results in Atlanta which turned out to be a cyst. She explained that most women my age were happy to have firm breasts. I kind of laughed at the fact that she threw my age into the conversation, but that statement alone caused me to be alarmed. I told her that I felt like I needed more testing because the mass was so hard. I showed her the small scar on my right breast from the three biopsies over the years. I told her my family history again and about my sister who currently had breast cancer. To my surprise, she was not happy that I would not take her word regarding the results. She went out and came back with the news that the manager said to give me a 3D mammogram, if I were willing to pay for it in case my insurance didn't cover the fee. After the 3D mammogram, she gave me the same dense tissue report and looked very proud that she was right.

Now that I look back on that day, I realized that her unprofessional behavior was also God sounding the alarm for me. That is exactly what happened. If she had been nicer, I don't know if my frustration with the results would have grown so fast. I pushed back on what she was saying about the results from the 3D mammogram and asked for her manager. The manager never showed her/his face but did ask the radiologist to do what she referred to as an ultrasound. After the ultrasound, the radiologist came back and gave me the same results. She said, "Miss... you have very dense tissue. You are just fine and we will be sending you the results in writing in a few days. We will also send a copy to your doctor, if their information is on file." She had this proud look on her face because she thought she was right and how dare I question her. I was not buying a word she said at that point.

When I left the office, the young lady at the front desk could see that I was not okay and she said, "It's going to be fine. Your results will be sent in writing as soon as possible." Her smiling face helped my heart but not my health. I didn't believe I was okay. The alarm was on now and I could not turn it off. I called Dr. Rothman's office the same day and told the receptionist about my experience with the radiologist. The receptionist gave Dr. Rothman my message. He instructed her to make me a second appointment with him in about 10 days, by which time he should have received the letter.

Two weeks later we both received the following letter:

ASSOCIATION OF ALEXANDRIA RADIOLOGISTS, PC

4660 Kenmore Ave. Suite 525
Alexandria, VA 22304
(703) 751-5055

SHELIA MOSES

Dear Patient:

We are pleased to inform you that the results of your recent breast imaging examination dated 04/30/2015 are *normal/benign* (not cancer).

A report of your results was sent to:

Your images will become part of your medical file here at AAR and will be available for your continuing care. You are responsible for informing any new health care provider or breast imaging facility of the date and location of this examination.

In compliance with newly enacted Virginia law and standards put forth by the American College of Radiology we must inform you of the following. Your mammogram demonstrates that you may have dense breast tissue. Dense breast tissue is very common and is not abnormal. However, dense breast tissue can make it harder to find cancer on a mammogram and may also be associated with an increased risk of breast cancer. This information is given to you to raise your awareness. Use this information to talk to your doctor about your own risks for breast cancer. At that time, ask your doctor if more screening tests might be useful based on your risk. A report of your mammography results has been sent to your referring physician's office. You should contact your physician if you have any questions or concerns about this report.

Although mammography is the most accurate method for early detection, not all cancers are found through mammography. A breast finding of concern should never be ignored despite a normal mammogram. If you notice any new changes in your breast(s) you should bring them to your health care provider's attention immediately.

Thank you for allowing us to help in meeting your health care needs.

Sincerely,

RAMESH RAO, MD

American Cancer Society Guidelines for
Early Breast Cancer Detection in Women without Symptoms

Mammogram: Yearly mammograms are recommended starting at age 40 and continuing for as long as a woman is in good health.

Clinical breast exam: Clinical breast exams should be part of a periodic health exam – about every three years for women in their 20s and 30s and every year after for women 40 and over.

Breast awareness and breast self-exam: Women should know how their breasts normally feel and report any breast change promptly to their health care providers. Breast self-exams are an option for women starting in their 20s.

Breast magnetic resonance imaging (MRI): Screening MRI is recommended for women with an approximately 20-25% or greater lifetime risk of breast cancer, including women with a strong family history of breast or ovarian cancer and women who were treated for Hodgkin's disease.

In my opinion, this letter is a death trap. The reason I stand by calling this letter a death trap is that if I had gotten excited and stopped at the relief of "not having cancer," as stated in the first sentence, I would not be here today. In the next paragraph they state the new Virginia law which requires them to inform you that dense tissue makes it hard to find cancer. That whole paragraph is dangerous. It should read, "YOU HAVE DENSE TISSUE AND WE HIGHLY RECOMMEND THAT YOU FOLLOW UP WITH A BREAST SPECIALIST IMMEDIATELY." Instead, it is just a paragraph WARNING YOU about dense tissue.

Dr. Rothman examined the area of concern again when I went back for my second visit. He was not going to leave me hanging with that letter knowing my family history. "Young lady, I hope that this is nothing, but you are the most persistent patient I have ever dealt with and that is a good thing. I know a great breast specialist named David Weintritt. Let's see how soon he can see you. He is one of the best breast specialists in Virginia, if not the country." Dr. Rothman had his assistant call Dr. Weintritt's office and ask them if they could fit me in. By now it was mid-May and they could not see me until the end of May, but that was the best I could do at the time. Those two weeks felt like forever.

I didn't say anything to anyone in my family because we were all very worried about my sister's condition. She had been fighting breast cancer for four years and was not doing well at all. The last thing I wanted to do was worry them. I wanted to be wrong about the mass. On the other hand, I didn't believe I was okay. I had to follow my instincts. I want everyone reading this book to remember: *Follow your instincts.* If you feel that something is not right, don't stop until you prove yourself wrong. That is what I did.

While I was waiting to see Dr. Weintritt, God continued to send me signs to make sure I kept my appointment. The weekend after seeing Dr. Rothman, I went to Greensboro to my nephew's graduation. After his graduation, I went to my great nephew's first birthday party. When I arrived, his mother, Crystal, kept looking at me.

She said, "What is going on with you, Auntie? I just saw you in March and you looked great! You don't look like you feel good at all." She was referring to seeing me in my hometown for a rally for our brother, Daniel McCoy Moses, who went missing in 2011. My brother's disappearance is a whole separate story and the sorrow of my life.

Crystal was right about seeing me on March 15, 2015, and I was just fine. That's how quickly my life changed. She continued hounding me all day. A year earlier she had a life-threatening health scare and I truly believe she felt the bad energy of sickness around me. She asked me several times if I was okay and she just would not let it go. That was God once again letting me know that something was wrong.

At the end of May 2015, I was on my way to see Dr. Weintritt. His office was located on the lower level of Alexandria's Mount Vernon Nova Hospital at the time. The women at Dr. Weintritt's office greeted me with a smile. They served me tea in a pretty cup and made small talk until it was my turn to see Dr. Weintritt. I only had to wait about 15 minutes, but it felt like an eternity. I was watching the patients leave one by one and studying the expressions on their faces. I could identify the ladies who had gotten good news versus the women who were battling cancer. I could see the fear on their faces. I whispered a prayer for them: "Yea, though I walk through the valley of the shadow of death, I will fear no evil."

I pulled myself back together when the nurse called my name. Another nice lady led me to the examining room and Dr. Weintritt came in immediately. First of all, he was physically one of the best-looking men I had ever seen in my life. I was tickled because he distracted me from the reason I was there. I still laugh about that.

His good looks were at the bottom of the list of what a fine person and doctor, he turned out to be for me. He asked a thousand questions because Dr. Rothman had sent him a message about my family history and my sister's current condition. Dr. Weintritt wanted the full story and did not rush me. That was so important because he was showing me that he was not only a good doctor, but he cared. He asked me to undress from the waist up and asked his nurse to bring in the equipment for a sonogram as he stepped out of the room.

When he came back in the room, he continued to ask questions about my family history as he did the examination. My eyes went back and forth between his face and the vision on the screen. He didn't look alarmed at all, but he wasn't smiling anymore.

"Ms. Moses, I am glad you came in. I do see a small mass. I want to do a biopsy as soon as possible. If you have time, I will do it now." The fact that he didn't want to wait was not scary; it just showed me that he was a good doctor like Dr. Martin back in Atlanta. Dr. Martin always let me look when she did the needle biopsy. It was always round, almost like a marble. This time, I saw a mass shaped almost like an airplane. It was not round at all.

"Yes, let's do it now," I said to Dr. Weintritt.

There was no time for me to call a friend to ask them to be with me. Actually, there were not a lot of people to call. My sister Jackie lived in Maryland, but she was at work, and my friends lived across the bridge in D.C. I had a lot of associates in Alexandria, but I had left my ride-or-die friends behind in Atlanta. I was starting to meet new people in my neighborhood, but I didn't call them either.

When Dr. Weintritt finished the biopsy, he told me to try not to worry and he would be in touch as soon as possible. My biopsy was on the Thursday before Memorial Day. That meant I would have to wait at least until Tuesday to get my results.

That weekend I traveled to Richmond to visit my sister who was now very ill. I remember sitting on the couch with her in the family room of the house she loved so much. I didn't say a word to her or anyone else, but God spoke to me. "You both have cancer. Go home and fight. You have to fight."

I rushed back home that Sunday, changed clothes and went over to my great niece's graduation party in Maryland. I am so glad I took a picture with my niece, Tarsula, and her daughters Brittany and Destiny: It was the last photograph of me before my cancer was confirmed, and probably the last time I smiled without forcing myself to do so for a very long time. It was not the beginning of the end, but it was definitely the last picture of me when my life was normal.

I honestly don't remember what I did that Monday, but I remember thinking that Dr. Weintritt was going to call the next day. Hours went by on Tuesday and finally around 4:30 the phone rang and it was his office. I remember exactly what street I was on as I drove to Costco. The young lady in his office asked me to hold for Dr. Weintritt. Well, if the news was

good, she would have just told me, so I pulled into the bank parking lot and waited.

Dr. Weintritt's voice came on the telephone line. "Ms. Moses, I have your test results and you need to come in as soon as possible."

I took a deep breath. "No, I don't need to come in. You can tell me on the phone."

"I would prefer you come in," he insisted, as I insisted again that he tell me over the phone.

Dr. Weintritt paused.

"Well, this is a first, but you are right. You do have breast cancer. You have the same type as your sister. It is triple negative breast cancer and likely stage 2, but that is for your oncologist to determine. I will make a referral when you come back in to see me. This cannot wait."

"Okay! I'll call back shortly to make an appointment."

"Ms. Moses," he said.

"Yes?"

"You did well! Early detection is very important. I will see you in a few days."

I hung up and tried to pull myself together. It was June 1st and very hot. I just sat in my car and never made it to Costco. I didn't call any of my siblings and I was definitely not going to call my mother who was 89 years old at the time. I had no idea how I was going to break the news to them that another sister had breast cancer.

I dialed Dr. Weintritt's office again and made a new appointment, and then I called one of my friends in Atlanta, Kim Abnatha. I rarely lose my cool, but I did that day. It was the first and only time in the last eight years that I just could not control myself.

"It's going to kill us all," somehow came out of my mouth in between screams as Kim tried to calm me down.

I also think that it was the first and only time I spoke negatively about my life as a person with cancer. I knew better than to speak negatively of any situation. He is with our ancestors now, but I will always be a student of Dick Gregory. One of the greatest lessons he taught me was, "Never give your power to your enemy. If you entertain your enemy, you give the situation or that person your power."

I had just met my enemy! Breast Cancer!

CHAPTER 2

FEAR

Real friends are the next best thing to family. I remember Kim praying with me on June 1, 2015. I remember the tone of her voice when she told me that God was going to take care of me. I calmed down because somewhere in between my tears, I believed her. I was still afraid, but I believed her. Most of all, I believed, and still believe, in God! My mind was racing all over the place as I told her I was okay before starting my car to drive home.

I didn't call anyone else when I got home. I wasn't ready to tell my family that not one but two siblings had breast cancer. Even though I was not shocked by the results, just hearing the words "You have cancer" changed my life forever. Let me assure you that thinking something negative is happening to your body is totally different from knowing for sure. It's completely different from hearing the ugly six-letter word. CANCER!!!

I turned on my computer and started to google different cancer websites. That is what I had been doing for years after we received the news from my sister about her cancer. If she sent us a medical update via email, I would research the medical terms and then I would pray for God to heal her. Now,

I was praying for both of us. It was a mistake for me to start searching the internet that night. The reason you should wait is… anything negative you can imagine about triple negative breast cancer, will show up before information that could be helpful or positive. To give you an accurate definition of triple negative breast cancer, I used the official TNBC website (see appendix).

I learned over the years to always refer to the Triple Negative Breast Cancer website because some of the websites have the wrong information. Scary information! I think what scared me the most was the information about lymph nodes. According to the Triple Negative Breast Cancer website, if the cancer has spread into nearby lymph nodes, the 5-year survival rate is 65 percent. If the cancer had spread further into the body, the rate is 12 percent. Of course, I could only see the lowest percentage as I continued to read. Five years! I was turning 54 in a few weeks.

That night, I had a light bulb moment. All those years I had dealt with the cyst in my right breast had been teaching me what to do when breast cancer invaded my body. There is no way that waiting until I was 40 to start getting mammograms would have been the right medical decision for me. I will keep saying throughout this book that I am not a doctor, so the following is my opinion. My opinion is that you should start getting not just a mammogram but a sonogram in your early thirties. Remember, I found my first mass in my right breast at age 32. The other reason is that women of color have a 40 percent higher chance of getting triple negative breast cancer than white women. Women of color under 40 are more likely to be diagnosed with breast cancer than white women. And don't forget that my niece lost her battle with breast cancer at the age of 34. So, waiting until I was 40 years old for my first mammogram would have meant a cyst lying dormant in my body for nine years.

All of these facts were running through my head on June 1, 2015. I continued to google different websites until around 10:30 p.m. I finally got tired and logged off. I prayed for a long time. Later that night I called the one person who I felt could help me.

"Girlfriend!" Dick Gregory said as he answered the phone. That is the nickname he called all of his female friends. He did not mean it in a disrespectful way. That was his way of acknowledging his feelings for the people he loved and the people who loved him. For 25 years we had been on a journey from me being his agent, to writing his memoir and him becoming one of my best friends and father figure. He was always there when I needed him.

"Hey Greg."

"Is that fear I hear in your voice?" he asked. That's how good he was at reading people. That's how tuned in he was to people he loved.

"Yes! I went to the doctor."

"And?"

"I have breast cancer."

Silence for a long time!

"God and fear cannot occupy the same space," he said in a calm voice.

I had heard him say those words a thousand times since I met him. When we met in the summer of 1992, he also told me that we met for a reason that had nothing to do with him and everything to do with me. I thought at the time that our meeting was for business reasons because I was an agent and searching for new clients. I also thought it was to teach me about the Civil Rights movement. When I stopped working as an agent and started writing full time, I just knew that I had met him to write his memoir. I was wrong! The reason was that God knew I would need the wisdom of Dick Gregory on one of the darkest days of my life. I thought about all of that as he continued to talk.

"In order for me to help you, you have to trust God and trust everything I tell you to do from now until you are cancer free. You must also get rid of the fear because it will cloud your judgment."

He continued to talk for 30 minutes. I didn't say anything. At the end of our chat he said, "Punch in 'black seed oil' when we hang up and we will talk tomorrow." Then he was gone.

When he used the term "punch in," he was referring to typing something on the computer to do research. That is still funny to me but I did "punch in" the words "black seed oil" and researched the product. I read about the benefits it had on the human body and the side effects (see appendix).

I didn't research anything else that night. I went to bed and slept better because I had shared my secret with two people who loved me. I was no longer alone.

The next morning the phone rang around 6:00 a.m. It was Dick Gregory.

"I called you to talk to you about the prayer of thanksgiving. I know I told you this before, but let me tell you again. When you pray, you don't have to beg God. Don't say, 'Lord, help me!' I need you to say, 'Thank you, God for my healing.' You must pray to him like it's already done. Pray like your prayer is already answered. Never beg."

From that day through today, when I pray, I always thank God for everything in advance. Whether it is small or something big happening, I thank God in advance.

After we talked about the prayer of thanksgiving, Dick said:

"You can beat this, but you have to listen to me. Take the medicines the doctors give you but there is another side to this thing that will help save your life. I will put you in touch with the best nutritionist in the world and I have a book for you. Switch to a plant-based diet immediately. Cut out all the pork y'all country folks eat. Here's the second thing I want you to do. When you pick up your black seed oil, pick up an organic lemon and baking soda. Make a large container of lemon juice and water. Each night before you go to bed, put one pinch of baking soda in a ceramic cup of lemon water and cover the cup with the saucer. The next morning you need to drink it before you eat breakfast."

He explained the effect of baking soda and lemon water on the human body. I listened to him and then I did my own research. I am not a holistic doctor so I am not making this recommendation to you. I am sharing with you what I learned (see appendix).

Dick Gregory was a unique person who was misunderstood by many people and beloved by even more. After we talked that morning, I knew for sure that with the exception of my almighty God, Dick Gregory's wisdom as a nutritionist was my best bet. The fight was on.

On Friday, I went back to see Dr. Weintritt. He went over the steps to beating triple negative breast cancer. He never mentioned living with cancer. He kept saying "beating cancer." He explained to me the difference between a breast specialist and an oncologist. He had two oncologists in mind for me to see as soon as possible. I don't remember the other doctor's name. He said that Dr. Soren Caffey's office was one block away from his office. I was listening to Dr. Weintritt praise Dr. Caffey and say how happy his patients were with him.

My first visit to Dr. Caffey was scary and funny. I didn't know that you keep your clothes on when you visit the oncologist, so I immediately removed my blouse and bra. He informed me that that his concerns were about what was happening on the inside of my body.

After I laughed and put my clothes back on, he explained what would happen next. He ordered a series of blood tests and a PET Scan. You should not have to do any of these things alone, but I was alone, as my sister's battle with breast cancer was ending along with her pain and suffering. There was no good time to tell my family that I had just been diagnosed with the same disease.

After a few days, I did what I have done since I was a little girl: I called my brother, Leon. He is four years older than I am and has always been my go-to person in the family. I think it's because he was the last brother at home and really thought he was the boss. Some people think they are the boss but don't have the skills of a good leader. Leon is a good leader and very compassionate. He was devastated but held it together while on the phone with me. His wife, Iris, told me that he was very upset when he told her and my cousin, Barbara Jacobs, later.

I was sad that I had to break my siblings' hearts but there was no way around telling them because I was preparing for chemotherapy. We have a lot of cousins but have always been very close to Barbara and her siblings. Their mother, Lucy is our first cousin and a breast cancer survivor. Barbara and her siblings rallied around us and showed up when needed. I was glad that they were there for Leon since he had to be the first to learn about my cancer. Between the two of us, we broke the news to our siblings one by one.

Now that my family and friends knew my situation, I turned my attention back to my health. I was preparing myself mentally for my PET scan. For each test, the fear would try to creep back in. I had to tell myself daily that God and fear cannot occupy the same space. Before breast cancer, I was never scared about anything. Ma used to say I was too hard-headed to be scared, but the thought of a PET scan scared me. Remember, in the blink of an eye I had gone from never spending one night in the hospital to being a breast cancer patient. I was also nervous about the PET scan because Dr. Caffey had informed me that this test would tell him the actual stage of my cancer.

My sister Jackie drove me to find the location on a Sunday afternoon so I would know exactly where to go the next morning. It was her turn to sit with my sister and I insisted that she go back to Richmond. She had to go; we all knew that every precious moment would count.

That Monday morning, I drove to Woodburn Center for my PET scan. I have had six scans since that time, but the first one was the worst, mentally and physically. The technologist escorted me to the cold injection room that made the fear set in even more. He was kind as he explained the steps of a PET scan to me. After starting my intravenous line, he administered the radiopharmaceutical injection. The next step after the sugar and radioactive fluids are going into your body is to wait in the dark. Those 75 minutes allow the radioactive material and sugar to absorb in the cancer cells so the cells become more visible. The technologist, who still works there eight years later, made small talk as he wrapped me in a warm white blanket like I was his sister and not a patient. For a split second, I forgot about my fears and enjoyed the warm blanket as he closed the door. Even when the blanket was cold again, I felt the warmth that a total stranger had left in the room. Most of all, I felt the presence of God as I prayed the prayer of thanksgiving.

When it was time to enter the room where the huge scanner was located, I tried to keep the same good energy I had had in the dark room where I had met a new friend. That was not as easy as I thought. That was the day I discovered that I was claustrophobic. I had always felt strange whenever I am on a plane, but I have never been scared to fly. Well, let me take that back. I was afraid to fly for about 6 months after the attack on America on September 11, 2001. I was so traumatized after 9/11 that I took a train from Washington,

D.C. to Los Angeles, California to avoid flying. I was living bi-coastal at the time so I just stayed in Pacific Palisades until March,2002. I had to quickly get over the fear of flying because that was the longest I had ever stayed away from my mother in my entire life. I eventually learned to suck it up with each trip. I would just have a glass of wine and move along.

There were no options for me now. I could not drink wine before my first PET scan, but I could trust God one more time. That is what I did. You are literally lying flat on your back and you can't move for 30 minutes. What came to me as I tried to pull myself together was one of my favorite books, *In the Meantime* by Iyanna Vanzant. I often read this book to remind myself that things are not always perfect. There are times that you are waiting for something to happen, but you can't just sit and wait. Iyana suggests that you do something positive while you wait. Do something productive! What is more productive than prayer? I prayed. Eight years later when I entered that large machine that would make an image of my body from the neck down, I just prayed: "God, I thank you for standing by me. I thank you for my healing." After I pray, I remember the words of Dick Gregory: "God and Fear cannot occupy the same space."

CHAPTER 3

LOSS AND TRYING TO SURVIVE

After my PET scan, I rushed to my car because I wanted to call Dr. Caffey's office. The office manager answered the telephone. I don't know what I thought she could do but I told her about my experience during my PET scan. I asked her when she thought I would receive my test results. I knew the results would be posted on my portal but I didn't know when. I now assume that she receives calls from patients just like me all the time because she was very calm and knew exactly what to say. I am sure someone from Dr. Caffey's office had explained the steps for a PET scan to me earlier, but she slowly gave me the information again.

"Ms. Moses, I want to suggest that you don't go on the portal and read your results. Wait until you visit Dr. Caffey. That is the reason we scheduled your appointment a few days after your scan. Your appointment is two days away. You will not have to wait long. We are not doctors. When you read your results early, you start doing research and try to do his job. Just wait until you come in. If you feel nervous, that is a natural feeling but please wait."

I am so glad I listened to her. You don't know what the results will be each time you get a PET scan. You can only pray for God to cover you and hope that everything will be okay. You just pray each time that you are cancer free. The worst thing you can do is read something bad or see information you don't understand on your portal and have to wait for the doctor to explain it to you. When I went back to Dr. Caffey, the news was not horrible, but it was not great.

"Ms. Moses, based on your blood work and your PET scan, this is not Stage 2 cancer; it is Stage 3. We should start your chemotherapy treatment immediately. Based on your family history it is not in your best interest to wait."

He explained that I would need eight rounds of chemotherapy and I would have treatments every two weeks. Starting chemotherapy on June 27th meant I could be finished the last week of September. Dr. Caffey scheduled me for chemo on Thursdays and neulasta injections the following day. Before starting chemotherapy, I would have to have a port placed in my chest over my right breast. Dr. Caffey didn't explain much about the port to me. Dr. Weintritt and Dr. Caffey were very careful about only explaining the areas of my treatment that they were responsible for. I found their method very helpful as time went on. Dr. Caffey told me that Dr. Weintritt would perform the outpatient surgery for my port, which should happen as soon as possible.

I already had my next appointment scheduled with Dr. Weintritt, so I only had to wait one day to discuss the outpatient surgery for my port.

I left Dr. Caffey's office and went to Costco. I just didn't want to go home. Everyone in my family was so sad about my sister that I decided not to call anyone. I just walked around the store and picked up things I would need on the days I didn't feel well. I purchased extra water, vegetables that I could cook and freeze, etc. I went to the bookstore and purchased a few books and a journal. From that day until I was cancer-free, I made notes about my health and my spiritual journey. Those notes are a big portion of the book you are currently reading.

Later that evening, I talked to Leon and a few friends. I really didn't want to talk to people who were offering all kinds of advice. I also called my sister/friend, Marie in St. Louis. Marie is a good listener and that is what she did that night. She listened. It was just too much to try to talk to everyone while preparing for chemotherapy. Most of them had never had cancer and were telling me things they read on the internet. I know that people mean well, but during that time I was careful about what I let into my head, heart, and body.

That was the loneliest I had ever felt in my life, but I was determined not to fall apart. I was not lonely because I didn't have friends or family. I was lonely because none of them could do anything to make the cancer go away. It was not a flat tire that a friend could come over and replace. This was cancer. When you think of cancer, you think of death. The rubber and the road had met and only God would save me. I had to turn off the noise.

Before going to bed, I did what I always did and called Dick Gregory. He was very firm as we talked.

"This is not going to be a joy ride. When the doctor told you that you had Stage 3 cancer, you were supposed to say, Thank God it's not Stage 4. Everything the doctors tell you, you have to remember that it could be worse. I know that's hard to do but you have to trust me. Most of all, you have to continue to trust God. Stop going back and forth. You trust God or you don't."

Dick was always blunt and straight to the point. He had no other way of communicating with people. You had to take what he told you and try to absorb as much as possible. I needed all of his wisdom to get me through. After he talked me off the cliff, Dick told me a silly joke, said "God bless you," and hung up without saying goodbye or good night. "God bless you" were always his final words in our conversations.

I pulled myself together and prepared for my next visit to Dr. Weintritt. When I went back, he explained the process and purpose of having a port. A port is a small device placed under the skin in your chest. The port is attached to a catheter that is threaded into a large vein above the right side of the heart called the *superior vena cava*. It sounds scary, but I was blessed to never have a problem with my port. Some people get infections, etc., but that was not the case for me.

After my visit with Dr. Weintritt I continued to read information on the Triple Negative Breast Cancer official website, information from the doctors, and Dick Gregory; most of all I prayed a lot. I talked to Dick as he reached out to some of the best holistic doctors in the world for me. I listened to all of them and then I would tell him what they told me. Not one of his friends charged me. Each one said, "Greg asked me to help you. Any friend of Greg's is my friend." I will never forget that.

As the days went by, I started to tell more people about my health situation. I had spent most of my adult life in Atlanta and had left my best friends in the world behind, but they called me daily. My friends Stephanie and Debbie would call me each morning to pray with me. If I didn't answer, one of them would leave a prayer on my voicemail. My friend Sandy is that ride-or-die girlfriend. She would hop on a plane and come just to look at me. Marie and her siblings rallied around me as much as they could long distance. No matter what family or friends did or said, there were still moments of silence that were lonely and scary. When those negative feelings tried to creep back in, I would pray even harder.

In between appointments, I was going to Richmond to see my sister who was on her last mile. My heart was broken for her and our family. I would sit with her and notice that she never complained. During one of my visits she had one request: "Take care of my boys!" That was it!

After our conversation, I came back to Northern Virginia because it was now time to have my port placement surgery.

That same night, Dick talked to me about how to protect my skin by using a product called Egyptian Magic.

"You should have never stopped using it," he said, referring to when I had used Egyptian Magic after the outpatient surgery to remove a lymphoma from my neck in 2000. The incision disappeared a week after my surgery and left the plastic surgeon in awe. I thought about all of that as I rushed out to get my Egyptian Magic and tried to prepare myself mentally for the outpatient surgery for my port.

Listen... No matter what anyone recommends to you, make sure you are put to sleep when you have your port placement. They gave me an option and I elected to have local anesthesia. Don't do it. I went through unnecessary pain. I had to quickly get over that pain because it was time for chemotherapy to start the next week.

Dr. Caffey is one of the few oncologists in the area who is also a chemotherapy provider. For whatever reason, my insurance company was fighting my having my treatments in his office and I was fighting back. Dr. Caffey insisted that I start the treatment at the hospital until my insurance company approved my treatments in his office.

When it was time for my first chemo session, my sister Jackie went with me to the hospital. She stood over me and prayed. There is nothing like watching them connect the equipment to your body with the medicine bags filled with medicines that can save your life but you know the side effects are brutal. As the medicines dripped into my body, I made small talk with Jackie. I can only imagine what she was really thinking with one sister starting her treatment and another sister gravely ill.

Dr. Caffey told me that some patients feel fine the first day of treatment and the next day the side effects start. That is exactly what happened to me.

Jackie spent the night with me. The next morning, we went back to the hospital to get my neulasta injection. She spent the day with me and then left for Richmond to see our sister because there was really no time left. We were all trying to see her as much as possible. Another one of my girlfriends, Kim Wilson, came and spent the second night with me. I will call that the night from hell. The throwing up, cramps and cold sweats are all real, but so is friendship. Kim stayed up with me all night. She has three beautiful children so she rushed home the next morning to check on them and came right back.

While she was gone, I called Dick and told him about my bad night. "Ask your friend to go to the store and pick up some raw organic ginger. Slice it up and boil it. After that you can drink it hot or cold but don't stop drinking it. Also, store it in a glass container, not plastic."

Research shows that ginger helps calm the digestive system. It will also help with nausea and vomiting. I was already using mostly glass containers, but after my cancer diagnosis, I threw away all of my plastic containers and replaced them with glass.

I called Kim and asked her to bring some ginger. Kim came back armed with food she had cooked for me and raw organic ginger. We made the ginger tea together. Afterward, we had a glass of iced ginger tea and a few laughs.

It worked! The ginger worked.

After Kim left that Sunday, I did little to nothing all day. I was fighting to get better because I had to get back to Richmond to see my sister one more time. I just had to. The time was so near that my family members were sitting with her around the clock, as my new friends tried to help me as much as possible.

Jackie and our sister, Gayle were sitting with our big sister day and night. When Jackie came home the next weekend, I decided to ride back to Richmond with her. I knew I could not stay because I had chemo in just a few days. When it was time to leave, I told my sisters and my brother-in-law, Ted that I was going back on the train. I went into Loraine's room and said goodbye. She looked at me and said, "That's a pretty blouse. I will see you later."

I hugged her and left.

The train ride home is like so many things that happened during the summer of 2015. A blur! I pulled myself back together one more time and prepared for chemotherapy. I can't remember the reason but Dr. Caffey had changed my chemo to Friday and my shot would be that Saturday morning.

My neighbor, Evelyn, went with me to chemotherapy at the

hospital and sat with me all morning. When I threw up, she held the bag and my hand. Evelyn is such a positive person. She smiled at me and made small talk as we drove home. After I arrived home, I was okay the first day just like my first treatment. Dr. Caffey had warned me that my hair would probably fall out right after my second treatment and I would be completely bald within a matter of days. My hair was the last thing I was thinking about. I was thinking about how my sister was doing.

I made it through that Friday night and was trying to keep my mind straight to get my neulasta shot the next day. My neighbor, Brenda, who was a nurse, was scheduled to take me to the hospital for my shot. I remember lying in bed that Saturday morning when I ran my fingers through my hair. In my hand was a handful of hair. I froze and thought about the fact I hadn't picked up a wig as planned. I had tried to stay very organized during my chemotherapy days but I really didn't want to wear a wig. That was the one thing I had put off doing; I was thinking more along the lines of head wraps, etc.

Within seconds, my phone rang and I saw Jackie's name on my caller I.D. I knew that our big sister had joined my ancestors. I answered and we talked for a few minutes. I told her I was okay and never mentioned my hair. When I hung up, I dialed Ma, but the line was busy so I called the only father I had.

As blunt as Dick Gregory was most of the time, my sister's death shook him up. He was very sad. "How is your mother?" He asked. I told him her line was busy so we just talked.

"Greg, I can't remember if I told Loraine that I loved her the last time we were together."

He started laughing really loud.

"There is no sane person in your life that can doubt your love. She knew."

Before I hung up, I told him about my hair.

"Girlfriend, I cannot save your hair. You could not save your sister, but you cannot stop fighting to grieve. If you start grieving, you will not make it. The grief will kill you. Pull yourself together, go to the funeral and call me when you get back. You are a soldier. It's time to battle."

That sounds so harsh, but he was right. If I had fallen apart, I would not have made it.

I laid in bed a few minutes and pulled more of my hair out and started stacking it on the dresser. Then it hit me. "I will be damned if I am going to lose my sister and my hair the same day." I went in the bathroom and used my fingers, not a brush, to wrap my hair. I put on the brightest scarf I could find and jumped in the shower. As I was getting dressed, I called Brenda and told her about my sister.

Brenda and her husband, Dr. McDonald, were waiting to take me to the hospital, but Loraine's friend, Beverly, called and told me to cancel riding with my neighbors. She was on her way to pick me up. I felt safe again when Beverly arrived. I felt like I was with family. Beverly went to North Carolina Central University with my sister Loraine and she was, and will always be, family to all of us. We talked about the good times as she drove me to the hospital. I could tell that she was very sad, but she was holding it together for me.

After my treatment, Beverly dropped me off at home and she went back home to pack. She decided to take me to Richmond because I was determined to go. My sister, Scarlett was with our mother.

I tried to get some rest until Beverly came back to pick me up. Then I decided to go out and buy a wig. Bad idea! The lady at the wig store was a big help. I showed her a picture of me and she found a wig that looked almost identical, but that is not the way to shop for a wig when you are going through chemotherapy. I recommend that you not go alone. Take a friend with you and make it about more than going bald. It's a new look and it's not permanent. Also, you should take your wig to your stylist and let her cut it even closer to your own hair style. I wore the wig home and just walked around like a zombie until Beverly came back.

Beverly's husband Lee drove their car and Beverly drove me to Richmond. I was not thinking clearly because I really should have stayed home until I felt better. I felt horrible physically, mentally and emotionally.

When we arrived in Richmond, the house was full, but everyone was calm. It didn't feel like my sister was gone, just that she was not at home. I spent the night in Richmond and I was not feeling well at all. The next morning, I didn't put the wig on, but put on one of Loraine's beautiful scarves instead. Somehow, I made it to my mother's house. She was broken but strong as I tried to pretend I was okay. I tried to hide how sick I was as she soldiered on like only a mother can do.

My hair continued to fall out if I even touched it. One day while Ma was taking a nap, I drove to the local library. I could feel my scarf slip off as I pulled into the parking lot. That's it! I don't have time for this! I went in the bathroom and pulled some paper towels off the roll and placed them on the floor. I removed Loraine's scarf and most of my hair came off with it. I sat on the floor and removed as much of my hair as possible, wrapped it in the towel, pushed it down in the trash. Then I went home to Ma.

The next day, my sister-in-law drove me to Rocky Mount and I picked out a fabulous black hat for the funeral. A hat my sister would have looked at and said, "Go girl!" She was so conservative but got a kick out of my fashion statements.

Dear God, I made it through my sister's service and prepared to travel back home. After a few days, I drove back to

Virginia. I wanted to be home with my mother but that was impossible.

I had a terrible cough and felt worse than I had felt since starting chemotherapy. I knew I had to get back to Dr. Caffey. I drove back to Virginia that Wednesday in a daze. My doctors and their staff took it so personally when my sister passed. They were so determined that I was going to make it. Dr. Caffey told me to come directly to his office. He didn't even bother to send me to my physician but sent me directly to hospital after listening to my lungs. Just as Dr. Caffey thought, the doctor at the hospital determined that I had bronchitis.

They sent me home with a prescription and put notes in the portal so that Dr. Caffey could see them. I called him and he made it clear that I could not have chemo on my scheduled date which was that Friday. That was a blessing because every part of my body and soul needed to rest. Even though I didn't have chemo that week, Dr. Caffey asked me to come in for blood work on Monday. He also wanted to check my lungs.

I was glad to see Dr. Caffey and he had good news! My insurance company had finally approved my chemotherapy treatments in his office instead of at the hospital. I was very happy about that. I loved the nurses at the hospital, but I wanted to be in one place physically and mentally. Before I left, Dr. Caffey repeated what Dick Gregory had said: "I am sorry about your sister, but she wants you to live. I need you to try to put aside your grief and fight."

That is what we did. I put on my armor from God and I fought. With every treatment, I became weaker. With every treatment my body changed. When I looked in the mirror, I felt like I was looking at a stranger. I just kept holding on!

By early August, it was time to start discussing my double mastectomy with Dr. Weintritt. He explained to me that it was now time to bring the third doctor into my health care journey. Third doctor? I was so confused. Until that day, I thought he would be doing my surgery alone. He explained that he did not perform the reconstructive surgery, should I make the decision to get implants. I was 54 at the time and I was not ready to become a breast less woman like so many brave women have done over the years. Because I wanted implants, it was time to add plastic surgeon, Dr. Ali Al-Attar to our team. That's what I had: a whole team of angels. Dr. Ali Al-Attar, Dr. Caffey, and Dr. Weintritt are clearly cut from the same cloth. Kind and general men who put their patients first!

Dr. Al-Attar's office was about 10 minutes away from me and he kept long hours at three locations. That was perfect for me because he never turned anyone away if they didn't mind coming in late or driving to his McLean office which was much farther for me. I didn't want to wait, so I took the 30-minute drive to McLean.

I am a girl who loves pretty things so I was happy to see his beautiful office with more smiling faces walking around. The first thing I noticed about him was that he, too, knew my full story. Dr. Weintritt had taken the time to tell him about my sister, just like he had done with Dr. Caffey. He didn't just write a referral, he told him my story. After we talked about my family history, he explained the reconstructive procedure. It would take Dr. Weintritt two hours, and it would take Dr. Al-Attar another three hours to perform reconstructive surgery. Five hours seemed like a long time and made it all more frightening. When I told Leon and Iris that it was a 5-hour surgery, they immediately said they were coming to Virginia.

I wrote down everything Dr. Al-Attar said as I now had to navigate four doctors because I still had to see my primary physician from time to time. I also realized that I could not think too far ahead. First things first! I still had two months of chemo left.

When it was time to go back to chemotherapy, I made the decision to go alone. I knew that I would be fine the day of chemo and would only feel really bad for one or two days after chemo. It was also at Dr. Caffey's office now and I was surrounded by people who were not only taking care of me but had become my new friends. Due to the bronchitis and missing one chemotherapy treatment, my final day would be October 8th, not the end of September. I didn't let that bother me. I thought about all the women I have known with breast cancer and how many times their chemo treatments were canceled due to a cold or anything that affected their immune system. I just prayed and settled into my routine for the next three months.

Chemo on Thursday at 10:00

Shot on Friday at 1:00

Saturday – Bedrest

Sunday – Rebuilding my body to fight another day by resting.

On Mondays, I always felt like my old self so I would get back into the world. For me that meant going to the grocery store for the foods I could eat, catching up on telephone calls and just trying to be normal. I was working on a project as a consultant and they patiently waited each week for me to feel better to even dial my number. Then I would wait for another Thursday to come. Every now and then, I would muster up the strength to go home to visit my mother.

By my fourth round of chemotherapy, my body was going through all kinds of changes. However, I was talking to other women and realized that most of them were so much sicker than I was. I was grateful for that even on my worse days. I continued to do everything Dick Gregory suggested and only ate the meals I cooked from the cookbook Dick Gregory had given me. Make sure you pick up a copy of *The China Study All-Star Collection* by Leanne Campbell, PhD. The plant-based recipes are simple, inexpensive and taste really good. I also stopped reading, texting, etc., when I was receiving chemo treatments. Instead, I would try to fall asleep immediately after praying. No distractions. No thoughts about anything other than healing.

I was so happy on the morning of October 8th. I thanked God for my last day of treatment and prayed that I would never enter that room again. I had heard about how patients rang the bell and celebrated you when you completed treatment, but that did not happen on October 8th. I have never asked why but there was no bell ringing at Dr. Caffey's office.

When I arrived home, I had a beautiful basket of fruit waiting for me from author and friend Sharon Draper, flowers from my old love, and another big basket filled with apples from the Gregorys. The gifts touched my soul because I had no idea that people were actually keeping up with my chemotherapy schedule.

A week later, I was back in Dr. Caffey's office after having a CAT scan of my upper body. He had decided to wait until after my radiation treatments for another PET scan.

"Ms. Moses, the chemotherapy has served you well. There is only a small trace of the mass left in your breast. You still have cancer but the mass is very small. We can barely see it. It is my strong opinion that a mastectomy is necessary for your left breast and that is what I recommend you do as soon as possible. You have to wait 30 days after chemo but don't put this surgery off. There is no medical evidence to prove that having both breasts removed will prevent the cancer from returning. It is a decision you will have to make. I want you to also discuss this with Dr. Weintritt."

Dr. Caffey told me to focus on my mastectomy for now and he would see me in November after my surgery. Let me tell you something: I was feeling some kind of way about not seeing Dr. Caffey for a month. I had come to rely on him and his staff, both professionally and emotionally. In many ways, I still do.

It is mandatory that you wait 30 days or longer in between chemotherapy and any type of surgery and that was all I could do... wait. I had given up on trying to travel to do speaking engagements, so in mid-October, I decided to substitute teach on the days I felt okay. It was one of the best decisions I made during that time. If you want to forget about your problems, all you have to do is surround yourself with young people.

So, each morning, I would get up and walk to the school in my neighborhood. Lucky for me they had a long-term position available. It was a detention school, so I only had about eight students per class, and they were a blessing to me without even knowing it.

The principal was a very difficult person to get along with but he treated me okay. He was not nice to other teachers and that was stressful. I made friends with the teachers and we are still friends today. I survived chemo and they survived the principal from hell.

CHAPTER 4

A DOUBLE MASTECTOMY

After my chemotherapy treatments were over, my health and wellbeing were under the care Dr. Weintritt and Dr. Al-Attar. I was grateful but I felt like I was on a roller coaster at that point. Keeping up with the doctors and their exact roles in my healthcare was a full-time job. The two things that helped me stay on track were taking very good notes and that all my doctors were part of the Nova Health Care System. That meant the doctors didn't have to rely on me to tell them what was going on with bloodwork, future surgeries, etc. They could log into their portal and see my medical records. When I had bronchitis, the doctor at the hospital didn't have to ask me anything about my chemotherapy because it was all there. Not only did I try to get to know all my doctors, but they also knew each other.

When I met with Dr. Weintritt after my final chemotherapy treatment, he had read the notes in my file and consulted with Dr. Caffey about our next plan of action. Dr. Weintritt told me that it indeed was my decision if I wanted both breasts removed, but the left breast should be removed as soon as possible. I didn't give any thought to keeping my right breast. I had made the decision from day one that I would have a double mastectomy. Again, there is no medical proof that having a double mastectomy would lessen the chance of the cancer coming back. I felt would better serve me and enable me to sleep at night to have the double mastectomy. After a long talk with Dr. Weintritt, we set the surgery date for November 18, 2015.

Once again, I was waiting. Teaching was my saving grace even on my bad days because I had something to look forward to daily. When it was time for my surgery, the new principal gave me a box of candy, a big hug, and told me to come back when I was feeling better. The two male teachers on my end of the hall rallied around me like I was their sister. They were a testament to how we as human beings do not know where we will find love and blessings. Eight years later we are still friends. I still run into my students who are now out of college and they have long forgotten why they were ever placed in the detention center. They scream from car windows and I run into them at church and in the grocery store. One day last year, I was walking out of Starbucks and one of my former students came running across the parking lot. I recognized him immediately. He looked great and was doing well!

"Miss M, Miss M! I am so glad to see you! You made it! You made it!"

He went on to tell me how he and the other students were worried about me. They wondered what had happened to me after he graduated and went off to college. That encounter blessed my entire soul. I cried tears of joy when he walked away. People like my students were praying for me and I didn't even know that in 2015. I was so focused on getting ready for my double mastectomy; I could not see the army of angels around me.

God protected me and he sent his angels to watch over me. I didn't have to know they were there. God knew! Their love and prayers helped prepare me for surgery.

Instead of feeling sorry for myself the day before my double mastectomy, I spent the day getting organized. I knew I would not be coming back home after my surgery but I wanted my place to be spotless when I returned. I cooked my favorite meals and froze as much as I could.

Jackie came over that evening and spent the night with me. We packed my little bag for the hospital, plus a big bag for her to take home with her since I would not be able to stay at my home for a while. I would be staying with Jackie and her girls in Maryland. Just like they promised, Leon and Iris, came to be by my side.

Jackie and I arrived at the hospital early. The young lady at the registration desk called me to the back before Leon and his wife had arrived. Dr. Weintritt stopped by and went over the procedure with me again. Even though Dr. Al-Attar wasn't scheduled to come in until much later, he stopped by the hospital and talked with me too. Just before the anesthesiologist put me to sleep, they allowed Jackie to come to the back for a few minutes. We prayed together and just like that, she was gone. I was now asleep and on a five-hour journey that forever changed my body. I was in God's hands and those of some of the best doctors in Northern Virginia.

I woke up six hours later. Five hours of surgery and one hour of trying to wake up from a long deep sleep. The first words that came to my mind were, "The Lord kept me." Then I remembered feeling like a ton of bricks were on my chest. Dr. Al-Attar had explained the procedure regarding getting expanders after a mastectomy to keep your skin stretched until it was time for my actual implants, but I was shocked at how bad they made my upper body feel.

I reached down and touched my expanders. I touched the four surgical drains that were hanging from my body. The doctor had placed them on my stomach and I felt like an octopus. Surgical drains are very important after a mastectomy because fluid can build up in the area where your breast once made you feel beautiful. This build-up of fluid is not only painful but it slows down your healing. You can also develop what is known as a seroma which is a large amount of fluid build-up in one spot that can create scarring. So, there I was, both breasts gone with four long tubes hanging from my body with a surgical drain at the end of each tube. The room was cold and life was supposed to be sad, but I remembered how glad I was to be alive. I kept thanking God and I would hear Ma's voice in the kitchen the way I did early in the mornings when I was a child. When she finished a song, she would talk to God and say, "The Lord kept me from all hurt, harm, and danger." I repeated

Ma's words over and over again.

A few minutes later, Dr. Al-Attar came into the recovery room. He told me the surgery had gone well and Dr. Weintritt had been able to remove the cancer and two of the lymph nodes for testing. I was still very sleepy from all the medications and I don't remember his saying I was cancer-free, nor was that his job. Hours had passed since Dr. Weintritt had finished his part of the surgery, so he had left the hospital. Al-Attar assured me I was going to be okay and Dr. Weintritt would be back to talk with me.

After he left, the nurse allowed my family to come in. Leon looked so happy to tell me that Dr. Weintritt had told them immediately after my surgery that all the cancer had been removed. I don't remember anything else they said. I tried to eat some soup but I threw up.

My family members were only allowed to stay a few minutes and I was glad. I have always been a protector, and I really didn't want them to see me in pain. My mouth was moving and I was talking to them, but I was screaming inside. I knew that they were a telephone call away but I wanted to ride out the storm alone. The painkiller would take care of the rest.

A few hours later, I woke up again and I was fully awake this time in my room with Leon, Iris and Jackie. We talked a little while and I told them to go home and get some rest. Two of my friends walked in as they were leaving. We chatted a little while and then I ran them home too.

The first night was tough. No medicine can really ease that amount of pain but you have to know that joy will come in the morning. I just kept feeling like someone was pulling on my body and I could not get comfortable.

I finally fell asleep. For the first time in my life, I had a dream about my Aunt Fannie who had died in 2004. It wasn't just a dream, but I could not put together exactly what was happening. I remember her voice saying, "Pat, push your knees up."

The nurse came in at some point during the night and took my blood pressure and helped me walk to the bathroom. That was my first time getting up. I was thanking God for letting my feet touch the floor again. The nurse also made sure I knew how to release the fluid from the surgical drains. It was pretty simple: You had to pull the little balloon-shaped drain away from the tube and flush the liquids. Sounds gross, right? It's really not! It's survival.

After the nurse helped me get back in bed, it hit me what was happening. "Oh my God," I thought to myself. Aunt Fannie always slept with her knees bent and we thought that was so funny when we were kids. I bent my knees upward when the nurse left the room and I could not believe it. The pressure on my chest didn't go away, but it felt so much better.

When the nurse came back to check on me a little later, she asked, "Why are your legs up like that?" Somehow, I had managed to get one of the pillows from under my head and put it under my knees. I told her about the dream and she looked at me like, "Girl, you better get off those pain pills quickly." I wasn't thinking about what the nurse said. I was thinking about my ancestors. It was all so clear. I don't believe it was just a dream. Aunt Fannie had come back to see about me.

Later that morning, Dr. Weintritt stopped by to visit me. He explained what he had told my family the day before. "We were able to remove all the cancer from your body. I removed two lymph nodes to have them tested."

"Does this mean I am cancer free?" I asked.

"It means that you no longer have any visible cancer in your body. I will need you to come back to see me for a sonogram, but Dr. Caffey will do more bloodwork and order another PET scan to determine if you are totally in the clear. You should be very encouraged." His words meant everything to me because I just needed a little bit of hope. Dr. Weintritt left and I went back to sleep thanks to the pain medicine.

When my family arrived, I told them that I had dreamed about Aunt Fannie coming to visit me. I doubt if any of them thought that was strange at all. She was a force in our family and if anyone would come back to help me in any form or to represent the Jones clan, it would have been Aunt Fannie.

We started talking about other things and I was happy to be able to laugh a little. When you are "in the valley," you can't just talk about the valley. You have to look to the heavens and talk about the beautiful sky.

Jackie lived almost one hour away when the traffic is bad and I used that as a way to run them off again. I really just wanted to sleep but that did not happen.

Just like I knew he would, Dick Gregory had someone drive him to the hospital. For 25 years, he had shown up for every important event in my life. He had not just been a father figure in my life but a good father. He had on a baseball cap as usual but black folks who worked at the hospital recognized him immediately. Being the comedian, he was, he played it off and told the staff his name was Barack Obama.

For about one hour, he just sat there. Dick Gregory was never quiet. I asked him what was wrong.

"Nothing! I am here to teach you something. I want you to learn the power of silence when you are healing. I want you to know how they go hand in hand. Your body heals best when you are sleeping. I need you to sleep as much as possible. When you are feeling better, that is the time you battle to make sure you never have cancer again." He continued to explain the importance of sleep.

"There are many reasons why sleep is an important part of your physical and mental well-being." He described sleep as a shower for your brain. "While you are at work and school, your brain collects harmful waste proteins. When you are asleep, those harmful proteins are washed away and prepare your body and your mind for the next day. Sleep also allows your mind to process what you have heard, seen and experienced all day. It has to decode and regroup. In order for this to work, seven to eight hours per night are required. It's not a myth that you need eight hours of sleep. Getting less than eight hours of sleep leads to a worn-out immune system. So, there you have it. Sleep is how your body restores the power God gives you to carry on. It is the single most important daily habit you should have."

He had told me the power of sleep years ago, but I hadn't been using what he taught me. Now, I had no choice. From that day until now, anytime I feel bad, I take a nap. Then I get up and fight back. I am not always successful but I try to get eight hours of sleep per night. When I don't get the eight hours of sleep, I do feel the difference in my productivity the next day.

After Dick finished talking to me, he disappeared into the November air, leaving me encouraged that I could run another lap.

A few days later, Leon and Iris went back home and I was in the car with Jackie heading to her house for a week. That week was very hard. I slept most of the time and only got up to eat. I was very intentional about my sleep and my silence.

It was Thanksgiving weekend so I pulled myself together and went downstairs for dinner with my family. After dinner, I went back upstairs and fell into a deep sleep.

By Sunday, I was ready to go back home. I didn't feel 100 percent but all of my doctors were 10 minutes from me in Virginia. Staying in Maryland meant I had to take a one-hour drive every time I needed to see a doctor if the traffic was bad. Two of my neighbors were retired and they rotated with Jackie in the take-Shelia-to-the-doctor duties. I was grateful to have a sister nearby but I was also happy to be going home. I don't have stairs and that alone helped me feel better because each time I lifted my legs to walk up the steps, I felt pain in my chest area.

I was happy to be back home. Happy to be alive! I looked around my living room at the pictures for a long time. Pictures of my ancestors. My ancestors watching over me.

CHAPTER 5

RADIATION

I had no idea how long the road to recovery would be after my double mastectomy. Again, I was just happy to be alive.

Soon, I was in the driver's seat again and very excited to drive myself to see Dr. Al-Tarr, Dr. Caffey, and Dr. Weintritt. Dr. Caffey told me that, based on my bloodwork, I was cancer-free, but he still needed to order another PET scan after I completed the radiation. He recommended Dr. Grayson at the Inova Hospital on Seminary Road in Alexandria for my radiation treatment. Dr. Grayson is an oncologist who specialized in radiation treatment. I had one visit with her and then waited until January for my radiation treatments to begin. Dr. Caffey made the decision with Dr. Grayson that I would need 30 days of radiation.

There was so much going on all at once when I started my radiation treatment. Dr. Al-Attar was concerned and warned me about the effect radiation could have on my left breast. Radiation hardens the skin and, in some cases, can cause implants to harden, get infected, and totally fail. Along with Dr. Weintritt, they would monitor me and that was all they could do because there was no way around radiation. While waiting for my treatments to start, I continued my routine of eating plant-based food, drinking black seed oil and lemon/baking soda water, and rubbing my body down in Egyptian Magic daily.

I went home for Christmas and came back the next day. I didn't have the energy to pretend I was okay. Radiation was starting the first week of January and Dr. Grayson told me about the side effects. She warned me of how tired I would become over time, plus the darkening of the skin and longtime damage that radiation can do to the human body. Hearing all of this was just as scary as radiation but there was no turning back.

During the first week of January, I had one final visit with Dr. Grayson before my first radiation treatment. I stuffed my Egyptian Magic in my purse and told Dr. Grayson that I was planning to use it. She did not give me permission to use the Egyptian Magic, but she didn't tell me I couldn't. Instead, she prescribed a special cream for me to use. I picked up the prescription on the way home, but I made up my mind that I would use the prescribed cream on the days I had radiation treatments and Egyptian Magic on the weekends. I continued to follow doctor's orders, but also continued listening to Dick Gregory. I knew that only God would help me finish radiation without permanent damage.

My routine was the same for 30 business days. I would get up at 5:30 to arrive at Nova Hospital. It takes you longer to take off your clothes than it does to receive the radiation treatment, which only lasts a few minutes. After you are dressed in your gown, you are on the radiation table and then it's over. On the way out, you are treated with snacks, tea, and coffee.

There was nothing to like about chemo or surgery, but I disliked radiation more than anything I endured while trying to get well. I hated it because it was 30 days of the same thing. There was no way that it was good for my body. We will never know all the effects of radiation.

After the third day of radiation, I decided to return to teaching at the detention center. Each morning after radiation, I would drive to school and try to have a normal day. If I weren't teaching on any given day, I would have been at home writing or sleeping. Writing was almost impossible during that time because I was drained mentally and physically. Tired or not, when you are teaching, you have to be alert for the students.

Every Monday during my 30 days of radiation, I had to see Dr. Grayson. She encouraged me to not be discouraged by the fact that I had no energy. Dr. Grayson was amazed at how well my skin was doing during radiation. I wanted to laugh and tell her it was the Egyptian Magic. If you are reading this book, I am not telling you to use Egyptian Magic; I am simply telling you that it worked for me. My skin turned a shade darker, but that didn't last very long.

I did tell Dr. Al-Attar that I was not using the recommended products and he just shook his head and smiled.

Yes, I was happy with the results of my skin, but I was more concerned about what was going on inside my body versus outside. When Dr. Caffey received the results from my PET scan, he was so happy to confirm that the blood work was correct: The cancer was no longer showing in my body.

We discussed my next surgery to have the expanders removed, followed by surgery for my implants. He also told me that he recommended that I have a hysterectomy after things settled down from my implant surgery. Dr. Caffey was concerned about ovarian cancer and I agreed, but that was not my only reason for wanting the surgery. I had fibroid tumors that were huge and a hysterectomy seemed like the solution. The fibroids made my stomach big and made me feel horrible in my abdominal area. Dr. Caffey referred me to Dr. Scott Rose but I decided to wait a few months to even think about visiting him.

In the meantime, I continued the marathon of seeing my doctors. My new life was seeing Dr. Caffey every three months, Dr. Weintritt every six months, and Dr. Al-Attar every month. After radiation, I only had to see Dr. Grayson one time. I hoped and prayed that the radiation would not do internal damage to my body.

So much had happened in such a short period of time that I just could not think about having the hysterectomy in 2016. I also needed a moment to adjust to having my breasts removed and having my ovaries and uterus gone forever. The two things that some women see as their womanhood were not going to exist for me anymore. Well, my days of child-bearing were over, so there was no reason for me to mourn the loss of my ovaries. I just felt that it was a waste of energy to worry about my reproductive system. I needed that energy to fight another day. As it related to my reconstructive surgery, I knew I would not have perfect breasts, but I would be happy with what Dr. Al-Attar could do to make me feel good with or without clothes on. I continued to say the prayer of thanksgiving and maintained the gift of being grateful.

CHAPTER 6

WHEN THE STORM IS RAGING

In March of 2017, I started preparing for implant placement surgery. The original goal was to have surgery in November 2016, but I just didn't have the strength. Now I was finally ready.

Dr. Al-Attar warned me that because of radiation treatments, my left breast might not look the same as the right breast. He was working with a totally healthy right side of my body and a radiated left side. He told me he could not promise the left side would be okay but felt the right side would be just fine. What he was really saying was that the left side was hard from radiation and had damaged tissue. The implant could become infected and fail.

There was no need to discuss the risk with anyone other than my God, Dr. Al-Attar, and Dick Gregory. I prayed and kept my appointments with Dr. Al-Attar. I talked to Dick about my skincare and my diet. There was nothing else I could do.

To my surprise, the implant surgery was mild compared to what I had endured for two years. I was back up and about in a few days with little or no pain. I doubt if women love their implants after a double mastectomy, but I was happy to have the expanders out. I can say that Dr. Al-Attar did a great job, considering the radiation.

After I healed, I went to see Dr. Scott Rose regarding my hysterectomy. Dr. Rose is a great OB/GYN who specializes in fibroid tumors. He suggested a full hysterectomy and I agreed. During my second visit with him, I realized that I was burned out again from needles, doctors, etc. Another procedure just felt like too much. I wanted to put the surgery off so I discussed my decision with Dr. Rose. He would not let me off the hook and referred me back to Dr. Caffey. Dr. Caffey should have been a football coach because he sent me right back on the field. "You should have the surgery within the next year." That was the end of that!

I gave myself a break for a few months and set the surgery date for July 2017. During that time, I went to St. Louis for a speaking engagement. I was really happy about being back on the road again and I always loved working with the Missouri History Museum. My play, *I, Dred Scott* was making its debut in 2018 and I was excited. When it was time to leave, I noticed a rash on my arm. *What the heck,* I thought as I boarded the plane.

By the time the plane landed at Reagan National Airport, my arm was hurting and the rash had spread. I called my physician and made an appointment. The next day I was in her office. Shingles! I could not believe it! My physician explained that shingles generally is formed from the same virus that causes chickenpox. Once you have chickenpox, the virus can lie dormant in your body for years. It can be reactivated by illnesses that weaken your immune system, certain medicines, or stress. Not only is it contagious, but it is also very painful. Because shingles is contagious, my surgery was postponed for three weeks. I took the medicine my physician prescribed to me and rubbed my body down in Egyptian Magic every morning and night. Shingles often leaves scars but when it was over, I didn't have any scars and I was happy about that.

Three weeks later, I was back in the hospital with Leon, Iris, and Jackie standing by my bedside. My sister Barbara and her husband, Luke came to visit and I was happy to see them.

The hysterectomy had gone very well, but while in the hospital, I noticed that Dick Gregory did not call or stop by. Even though he was on tour, it was unusual for him not to call if he knew I was sick. I called his wife, Miss Lil, and asked if he were okay. She told me he was fine and the next day, I received flowers from her with a note that read, "Love Dick and Lil."

The flowers were beautiful but I just felt like something was not right. The following day Dick called. He always asked a lot of questions, but not this time. He was slow in his speech and just sounded really tired. The next day, I was looking on Facebook and I saw that he had canceled a gig in Atlanta. I knew that something was wrong so I called his nephew, Ferdy. He told me that Dick was not feeling well and was back in Washington, D.C. Even though he was 84 at the time, I just could not wrap my brain around him being sick. I was trying not to worry but I stayed in close contact with Ferdy. That is when I realized that Miss Lil had told me that Dick was okay because she knew I was in the hospital and didn't want me to worry.

Days went by and I continued seeing more cancellation notices popping up on social media. The doctor had not given me permission to drive, so I was trying to figure out how I was going to see Dick, who was now in the hospital.

On August 19, I called one of our mutual friends. He told me he would pick me up the next day and take me to the hospital. That sounded great but something kept telling me to get in my car and go to the hospital in Georgetown. I followed my instincts.

There he was! My hero! He looked frail but he was alert.

"Girlfriend, what are you doing here? Didn't you just get out of the hospital?" I assured him that I was fine. He really didn't talk much after that. Not only was he not talking, he didn't want anyone in the room to talk. Every time someone spoke, he would put one finger over his lips, signaling us to stop talking. It was almost as if he were listening to someone or something that we could not hear, and we were disturbing his peace.

When I got ready to leave he became very frustrated. Miss Lil had just arrived by train with their daughter, Paula. Some of the other children and Ferdy were already there so I wanted to give him time with his biological children and beautiful wife. I went to his bedside and told him I was leaving. He nodded his head and held my hand. Then he gave me a long look, the look that I now know was a long goodbye.

I called one of our mutual friends and talked to him as I drove back home. I told him I thought Dick was leaving us because nothing felt right.

I had not been at home five minutes when the phone rang.

Greg was gone!

Oh my God! He didn't want us to talk because he could hear God calling him home. He knew he was dying and I definitely felt it but I didn't think it would be that night. I rarely cry, but I did cry for my old friend.

I immediately called Leon. "I am sorry about Dick. I really am, but I need you to pull yourself together. You just had surgery and shingles. You can't afford to fall apart."

After we finished talking, I started walking around in my living room. I felt like I had to walk with Dick home to our ancestors. I finally grew tired and went to bed. I ignored my phone until the next morning when my sister/friend Dr. Jewel Faison called. Dr. Faison is very spiritual and wise.

Somewhere between my prayers and talking to Leon and Dr. Faison, it all made sense: What Dick Gregory had told me in 1992 made sense. We met so that he could pour his knowledge into me, the same knowledge he had shared with thousands of people. Some, like me, had a front row seat to history, and now he was gone.

Once again, God fixed it because Dick's funeral was put off until late September. This was just enough time for me to heal so that I could go and say goodbye.

Dick's brother, Dr. Ronald Gregory, came to town for the funeral and I spent most of the weekend with him, his wife, and daughter. After the burial that Sunday, Ronald walked me to my car. "You need to get some rest. You really don't look well." Like his brother, Ronald has good instincts because I was thinking, *Heck, I don't feel good.*

By the time I got home, I felt even worse. I texted Dr. Al-Attar and told him that my left breast was really sore. By Monday, I was in Dr. Al-Attar's office because I was physically turning red on my left side and I had a fever. He cut though the small talk.

"Take the antibiotics I am prescribing, but I don't like the way this looks. If it does not clear up by tomorrow, go straight to the hospital and check in. Tell them you think you have an infection and I will meet you there as soon as you call me. I am sorry but the only way to know what is going on is to make an incision and look for infection. I will not know if I have to remove the implant until I see what is happening in there."

I had survived stage-3 cancer, a double mastectomy, radiation, and two additional surgeries at this point. I was not about to give up now, nor was I going to worry.

I felt even worse the next day so I called Jackie and told her what was happening. She picked me up and we went to the hospital for emergency surgery. I had no idea if I would wake up with one breast or two. I just wanted to wake up; that was my prayer: "God, I thank you because I know you will get me through this surgery."

When I woke up in the recovery room, my left implant was gone! In all honesty, I was relieved. I didn't want to gamble and have an infection spread over my body. My new norm would be living with one breast or trying again later. I knew I would try again one day.

From September 2017 until September 2018, I just chose to have one implant. The left side of my body was tired. During that time, I decided to pour into my work. I went to Albany, Georgia, and taught a workshop for four weeks and started working on a new project. I wrote a history book about the legendary, W. S. Creecy High School in my hometown. I also wrote and produced a documentary based on the book and curated an exhibit. It was a project I had been putting off for years, and now it was perfect timing. I started doing speaking engagements again and going home more often to spend time with Ma.

Of course, it came with a physical cost to try to get back to normal professionally. The travel was brutal on my body. I started to notice swelling in my arms and hands. It was probably already there but I ignored it and/or attributed it to side effects from the reconstructive surgery. Dr. Al-Attar sent me to my physician and I was diagnosed with lymphedema and referred to physical therapy at a center in Lorton, Virginia. The physical therapist was really good and the therapy helped. She encouraged me to exercise more. Exercise was the one thing I was clearly not doing enough. I followed her instructions and started walking at least five days a week. I also wore compression sleeves and gloves that were custom made for me. Both helped. Every now and then I still have flareups, but it is minor compared to what other women and men have experienced.

After I was feeling better from the lymphedema, I had another hurdle to cross. The only way to have the left implant put back in was to have the expander put back in on the left side. I was not happy about that so I waited until April 2019 to have surgery. My goal was to wear expanders for about 6-8 months and then get a new implant.

My friend, Sandy drove me to the hospital. We made small talk and she encouraged me to believe that the expander would work this time. When she drove me home, she came in and sat with me for a while. I could tell she didn't want to leave. The surgeries and time were taking a toll on me, and she could tell. I did what I always did when she left. I prayed and slept.

I recovered faster this time from the expander placement surgery. Again, my goal was to only wear the expander for 6-8 months and get a new implant. At the end of December, I decided to wait until after the holidays. That was a mistake, or maybe not! I had no idea that the world was months away from a global pandemic.

CHAPTER 7

THE LAST MILE

After my reconstructive surgery for my expander placement, I kept up my routine of exercising, eating all the right foods and trying to stay positive. Dr. Ali-Attar set a March 2020 date for my new implant surgery. I was excited about what I prayed would be my last hospital visit. I felt better and stronger than I had felt in five years. I had no crystal ball to see that my life and that of the people around the world was about to change forever.

By early March, news reporters around the world started talking about a strange virus that had entered the United States. Within two weeks all hell broke loose. Schools across America were closing and hospitals were canceling surgeries unless it was an emergency due to Covid 19.

I had no problem with my surgery being put off because I could feel the danger around us. I was more concerned about Ma who was in a rehab center in my hometown. Neither Ma nor the other patients and staff knew the danger they were in. What was supposed to be a stay to help her walk better turned into a nightmare. Within one week everything shut down, including our ability to get Ma out of the rehab center because she had a fever. They would not allow us to visit Ma and we were crushed. I would drive to Rich Square from Virginia and get one of the nurses to Facetime with me so Ma could see my face. I could reverse my camera to show Ma that I was in the parking lot. I wanted her to know that I was there. I wanted her to know that only a wall was separating us. I would sit there for hours and then I would Facetime with her again. My heart is screaming as I type this paragraph!!!!

On May 26, 2020, my mother joined our ancestors. My heart was broken but I only have one regret. I still can't believe I was not allowed to be with her when she left this side of the mountain. I still can't believe that after she raised 10 children and doing the best she could for us, a virus had taken our right to be with her in the end.

After Ma's funeral, I spent my days at home, reading, writing and trying not to mourn too long. Ma was not one to mourn. When my biology teacher, Frances Clark, died, I was crying when Ma said, "Pat, Ms. Clark did what we all came here to do. She left here." She was telling me to pull myself together because life goes on.

When Aunt Rosie died a few years after Ms. Clark, I went home to stay with Ma for a while. One day she got up and said, "I am glad you stayed a while, but go home, child. Can't nobody replace her." That's how I felt when Ma died and will always feel. No one can replace her.

I understood Ma's words after she was gone. People live their lives and then they go home to be with the Lord. Their presence is not replaceable, and no one can help you grieve. I realized that I was not as strong as my mother. She had bounced back every time. She survived the Great Depression, the Civil Rights Movement, *and* raised 10 children. Now she was resting!

I continued to retreat at home for the summer of 2020. I was on a "stay at home vacation" with most of the world. There was no place to go in the middle of the pandemic as I watched the numbers rise from a few thousand to hundreds of thousands. People were dying!

With death all around all of us, I kept pushing. I had lost my dear sister and Dick Gregory. My big brother was still missing and now Ma was gone. I just had a made-up mind that I would not be broken.

In September 2020, hospitals were allowing doctors to perform non-emergency surgeries again. I was very nervous about simply going to the doctor's office, so I definitely didn't want to go to the hospital.

Dr. Al-Attar told me that we should move forward with my surgery because the virus numbers might go up during the winter months. Let me tell you something... I did not want to step into that hospital. It was a death trap for so many people during that time. Once again, I had to rely on my God and my faith.

The hospitals were still not allowing anyone to come in with patients unless you were accompanying a minor. That did not scare me because when they put you to sleep it's just you, God, and the doctors.

Sandy was more upset than I was that she could not come inside with me. She decided that she could sit in the parking lot during my surgery. She sat outside in the pouring rain and texted me every 30 minutes until it was time for surgery. When I woke up, she was still there, and my friend, Beverly was on her way. I told Sandy to go home because she had to drive back to D.C., whereas Beverly lived nearby. All masked up, I got in the car with Beverly and we were on our way home too. She tried to come inside with me, but I insisted that she go home. It was dangerous for her to be around me after being in the hospital all day. I was afraid that I would give Beverly the virus if I had contracted it in the hospital. By grace, I was fine!

That rainy day was my last time in the hospital. I refer to that day as the last mile. Since that time, I have had my good days and my bad. For the most part, I would say good. I eat healthily, I exercise, and most of all...I pray! I pray the prayer of thanksgiving and my mother's prayer: Lord, I thank you for keeping me safe from all hurt, harm, and danger.

APPENDIX

What Is Triple Negative Breast Cancer?

jodie.peters@acps.k12.va.usMany people do not understand that there are different kinds of breast cancer. Even some people who have had breast cancer do not understand the differences between triple negative breast cancers and breast cancers that are hormone receptor-positive or HER2-positive. People you meet may have taken a hormonal treatment pill for 5 to 10 years to lower their risk of recurrence (a return of the cancer), or they may know someone who has. These people may not understand that this option does not exist for you. Having to explain the differences between triple-negative and other breast cancers can be frustrating, especially if you are just learning about this diagnosis yourself. On the other hand, you may take some of the same chemotherapy medicines as other people with types of breast cancer.

SOURCE: https://tnbcfoundation.org/what-is-tnbc

WHAT IS A BIOPSY?

A biopsy is a procedure to remove a piece of tissue or a sample of cells from your body so that it can be tested in a laboratory. You may undergo a biopsy if you're experiencing certain signs and symptoms or if your health care provider has identified an area of concern. A biopsy can determine whether you have cancer or another condition.

Imaging tests such as CT scans or MRIs are helpful in detecting masses or irregular tissue, but they alone can't tell the difference between cancerous cells and cells that aren't cancerous. For most cancers, the only way to make a diagnosis is to perform a biopsy to collect cells for closer examination.

https://www.mayoclinic.org/diseases-conditions/cancer/in-depth/biopsy/art-20043922

What is a MEDI port?

A port is a device placed under the skin which connects to one of your major veins. It looks like a disc around the size of a quarter with a flexible tube attached. Ports can be made of metal or plastic.

Though they're often called "chemo ports," they're not just used for chemotherapy. Ports can be used to draw blood and deliver any other intravenous medication patients may need during treatment. They can also be used to infuse contrast solution for diagnostic imaging like CAT scans and MRIs.

On treatment days, you'll have your port accessed once, with a special needle stuck directly into the port. That way, if you need any additional infusions or blood draws, those can go through the port so that you don't need multiple needle sticks.

Having a port can make cancer treatment a bit more comfortable.

Just about anything that can be done through a traditional IV can be done through a port.

https://www.mdanderson.org/cancerwise/what-is-a-chemo-port-7-questions-answered.h00-159544479.html

Can Ginger Help During Chemotherapy Treatments?

Nausea and vomiting are common side effects of chemotherapy treatment for cancer. In most cases, these side effects can be managed with self-care measures and preventive medications. There also is evidence that when taken with standard anti-nausea medications, ginger may help further reduce or eliminate nausea and vomiting during and after chemotherapy treatments.

https://newsnetwork.mayoclinic.org/discussion/living-with-cancer-ginger-may-ease-nausea-and-vomiting-from-chemotherapy/

What effect does black seed oil have on cancer?

Black seed oil, also called black cumin oil, comes from the black cumin (*Nigella sativa*) plant and has been used for thousands of years in traditional medicine. Numerous studies reveal that black seed may be able to help fight and prevent all different kinds.

https://www.google.com/search?client=firefox-b-1-d&q=what+effect+does+black+seed+oil+have+on+breast+cancer#ip=1

Should you drink lemon water and baking soda after being diagnosed with cancer?

Lemon has already been proven to have strong anti-carcinogenic properties. In addition to this there are many other useful properties; lemon has a strong effect on cysts and tumors, and citrus fruit can cure cancer. Recent studies have shown that consuming citrus fruits, specifically lemons, have prevented and, in some cases, cured cancer. And by adding baking soda you will normalize the pH of the body which does not allow the cancer to continue to spread. A recent case-control study out of Europe showed that consuming four or more 150-gram portions per week of citrus fruit decreased the risks of throat cancer by 58 percent, oral/pharyngeal cancer by 53 percent, stomach cancer by 31 percent, and colorectal cancer by 18 percent. This study did not find a protective effect of citrus against breast cancer, but a recent American study shows that women consuming about 75 grams daily of grapefruit (fruit or juice) saw a 22% reduction of breast cancer risk if they had never used hormone replacement therapy. It is noteworthy that the protective level of citrus consumption was nearly identical in both these studies (525-600 grams per week) and could be interpreted as a minimum intake level for meaningful cancer protection. However, it's also important to know the best sources of limonoids if they are key to citrus fruit's anti-cancer properties. Lemon has a very strong antimicrobial effect with a very broad spectrum of activity against bacterial and fungal infections. Lemon is effective against internal parasites and worms, it regulates blood pressure and is a powerful antidepressant, reduces stress and nerve crises. What is the source of this information? It comes from one of the largest manufacturers of drugs, which states that after 20 laboratory tests conducted since 1970, they have proved that lemon destroys carcinogenic cells in 12 types of cancers. Lemon prevents the spread of carcinogenic cells and has 10,000 times stronger effect than drugs like Adriamycin, chemotherapy and narcotic products. Chemotherapy has horrible side effects, the worst being that it destroys healthy cells; simply put, it kills you. Lemon juice and baking soda, on the other hand, only kills the cancer cells.

https://www.met.edu/knowledge at met/lemon and baking soda a miraculous combination stronger than chemotherapy

YOUR NOTES